How To Be A Better Southerner
(Advice, Observations, and Inside Information)

Carolyn Kent

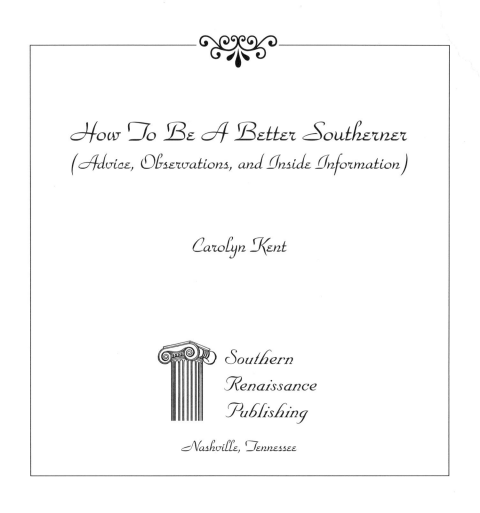

How To Be A Better Southerner
(Advice, Observations, and Inside Information)

Carolyn Kent

Southern
Renaissance
Publishing

Nashville, Tennessee

How To Be A Better Southerner
(Advice, Observations, and Inside Information)
by Carolyn Kent

ISBN-13: 978-0-9745160-0-4
ISBN-10: 0-9745160-0-7

Southern Renaissance Publishing
P.O. Box 160015
Nashville, Tennessee 37216

Dedication

To my parents, Elmer and Helen,
who raised their children with much love,
and in the traditions of the Old South.

Introduction

This book was written for all Southerners who celebrate their heritage. It was also written for those who are enchanted by the South, who seek to blend into the South, who are exploring the Southern mystique, and for those who really need help. For the many of us who were brought up in the traditions of the South the way of life is ingrained, but, in today's hustle it can use an occasional polishing. For those who appreciate the traditions but are still trying to "figure out the South," just relax, forget the analysis, assimilate and enjoy yourselves.

There are reasons this book was written and I shall share them with you. The South has always been, and still is, its own place. It is an area that has a presence and an atmosphere unlike any other on earth. It is a land of soft edges and dreamy colors, of soft-spoken people with the manners of nobility who have several times surprised the world by producing some of the greatest military minds and fiercest fighters on the continent. The South is a mix of contrasts and continuity, with a richness of right-living and, fortunately, a poverty of pessimism.

The people are a winsome blend of earthiness and aristocracy that lend a full spectrum to life. It is a place that is studied, discussed, written about, wondered about, and through it all, the South never gives up its secret . . . a secret that we, ourselves, have never defined. We are who we are, in part, because of the land, and we are also who we are because we have proven bloodlines that go back for centuries which harbor certain characteristics, and finally, we are who we are because our mothers said so!

Additionally, this book was written because the South seems in danger of losing its identity, of giving up the very things that make us different. In these days of homogenization, it becomes ever more difficult to hold on to what we are, who we are, and why we are. And yet, the world is entranced with the South, and probably we are entranced with ourselves, and we cannot let it go. To let "the South" disappear would impoverish the country of its grace and deny the world an inspiration.

So, others write, and I write, encouraging our people to keep our special place special. We are, as the magnolia, evergreen, straight and strong, but flexible, with our arms outstretched to the heavens in thanksgiving that our roots are firmly planted in Southern soil.

CAK, 2003

Always heed your mother's advice and mind your manners!

Keep your Southern accent . . . it's rare, precious and musical.

Avoid becoming too technical and automated . . . nothing enriches life like a face-to-face conversation where you can look into the eyes, or a hand-written letter to keep forever.

In spite of all the healthy food information, keep fried chicken in your life.

Gentlemen always open doors and ladies always thank them.

Attend local high school football games on autumn Friday nights. You'll see loyalty in its purest form and some good football.

In the South, don't misunderstand automobile turn signals. Don't assume that because the signal is *not* blinking that the driver is not going to turn – on the other hand, just because the turn signal *is* blinking, don't assume the driver is going anywhere but straight ahead.

Recliners being what they are, always own a rocking chair.

Know where "over yonder" is and be able to retrieve items from there.

Use magnolia branches to fill in gaps in your Christmas trees. They will stay as green as your trees throughout the season.

Learn your terms well. In the South, "making out" does not mean getting by during hard times.

Put family before all else but God.

Whenever possible, have a real fireplace in your house and use it often.

Steer clear of the politically-correct. They will bend your mind and warp your spirit.

Know why the original Natchez Trace was not a road but a path.

Create an opportunity each day to tell at least one person one fact of the true history of the South.

A Southern lady may practice yoga to relieve stress, but more likely, she practices bubble baths. This self-pampering ritual can be very elaborate . . . involving candles, taped music, a glass of wine or a cup of tea, and a favorite book. Indulgent? Maybe. Time-consuming? Possibly. Necessary? Absolutely!

The term "y'all" is plural. Period.

The Cavaliers of Olde England came to the South, while the rather dour Puritans went north. Is it any wonder we have more fun than they do?

Only in the South do we have "snow holidays."

Be aware that when people the world over fondly mention "Jack" from Tennessee, they're not referring to a relative or a mule.

Southerners have been called clannish, and yes, we are – most of us like our own groups very much!

A barn raisin' is completely different from raisin' the roof.

Be careful who you talk about in Southern circles . . . your subject is probably either related to or close friends of someone within hearing distance.

Have a firm handshake.

In the South, "laugh and the world laughs with you;" cry, and you'll get a handkerchief, a pat on the arm, and some sage advice about how to deal with whatever is troubling you.

Always say "yes, ma'am" and "no, ma'am" and "yes, sir" and "no, sir." Respect never goes out of style.

Southerners are very expressive . . . we never use one word when thirty or forty will do.

Always stand when *Dixie* is played, even if you are the only one. (Most of the time you won't be.)

Serve fresh homemade lemonade in the summertime. It's good for your body and good for your soul.

There is a continuity in the South born of tradition and a culture which goes back in time that is measured by centuries.

Be patient with little old lady drivers . . . someday you'll either be one or ride with one.

A Southerner is allowed to contradict her/himself in politics, religion and diet, but never in love.

Start a new old trend in your hometown . . . get majorettes back in the high school bands.

Be aware that the most burning question in any Southerner's mind is, "Where are you from?" (And given our history, rightly so.)

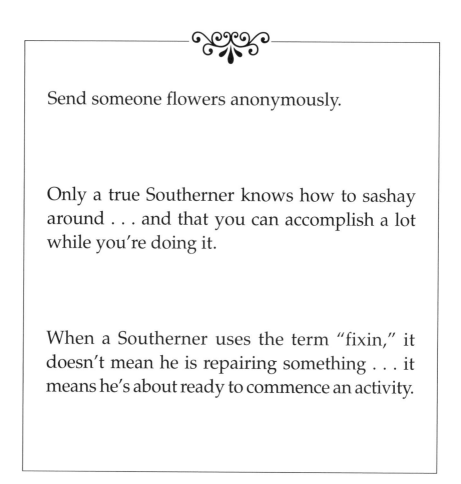

Send someone flowers anonymously.

Only a true Southerner knows how to sashay around . . . and that you can accomplish a lot while you're doing it.

When a Southerner uses the term "fixin," it doesn't mean he is repairing something . . . it means he's about ready to commence an activity.

Southerners rarely have identity crises . . . we know who we are!

It is the special "little touches" that make the difference between an ordinary occasion and a grand event.

Southerners may have unknowingly started the "endangered species" movement. After all, we've been protecting our dueling oaks for years.

To see perfection in the animal kingdom, attend the Plantation Horse Shows in Murfreesboro, Tennessee, or the Tennessee Walking Horse Celebration in Shelbyville.

A lot of old-time Southerners have never adjusted to half the hurricanes being called by men's names . . . . to them it's just a PC fad that washed ashore.

Be an unreconstructed Southerner.

The South was right! It still is!

Almost all Southerners have attended Vacation Bible School.

Molasses (called long-sweetening by the settlers) is amber, thick, clear, and about the best biscuit-topper we can think of.

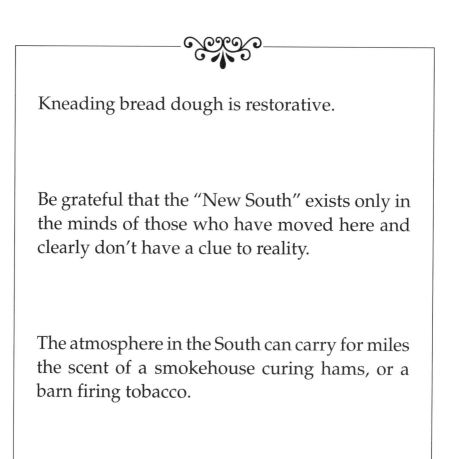

Kneading bread dough is restorative.

Be grateful that the "New South" exists only in the minds of those who have moved here and clearly don't have a clue to reality.

The atmosphere in the South can carry for miles the scent of a smokehouse curing hams, or a barn firing tobacco.

Only a yankee would address Dolly Parton, Faith Hill and Amy Grant as "you guys."

Learn all the verses of *The Bonnie Blue Flag* and always cheer when your state is mentioned.

Drive I-40 in Tennessee from lower west to upper east in the spring. The always beautiful scenery is enhanced by a display of dogwood and redbud in delicate pastels.

Gather fresh, wild blackberries as the sun rises and have them on your favorite breakfast cereal.

Drive I-40 in Tennessee from upper east to lower west in the autumn. The always beautiful scenery is enhanced by a display of fall foliage of astounding hues.

Record your children's voices with their natural, uninhibited Southern drawls, before the schools train it (shame it) out of them.

Volunteerism in the South is of magnificent proportions. It was once said that the ladies of Nashville could organize and color-code the world in a week's time.

Bring magnolia blooms into your house in season. The large creamy-white blooms enchant the mind and the senses with their beauty and fragrance. The magnolia is nature at its most elegant.

Pray often and mean it!

Kiss your family members good morning every morning and good night every night.

'Tis a poor farmer indeed that can't produce a few tomatoes by the first week in July.

Southerners have the best of all worlds.

In the South ambiance is everything!

You're a native only if you were born here; anyone else is referred to as "not from here."

On a cold and dreary winter's day, have an old-fashioned picnic, complete with fried chicken, baked beans, potato salad, pickled okra and chocolate cake, on a quilt in the middle of your living room floor. For added emphasis (and doldrum-lifting) play your favorite bluegrass or Beach Boys music. Wildflowers from the florist complete the atmosphere.

To be called honorable is the greatest compliment; to be honorable is the greatest virtue.

Adelicia Hayes Franklin Acklen Cheatham, of Belmont Mansion in Nashville, was a "belle" whose cotillions and soirees were so lavish and elegant, they are still talked about today.

Southern ladies know about white gloves . . . the very Old South ones demand white kid.

A true Southerner knows the difference between a violinist and a fiddler; also, the difference between a guitar player and a guitar picker.

Know that a "mess" has nothing to do with clutter.

If you think the Vanderbilt Fugitives are wanted by the law, then you need to visit your local library . . . the sooner the better.

Learn to ride a horse. No other ride gives you the peace and calm of horseback.

Southerners are always polite and gracious, but if you offend one of their own, gracious wrath can come down on your head.

The word "dang" may not be in the dictionary, but it dang sure is a part of the Southern vocabulary.

Never wear white before Easter or after Labor Day. Never wear velvet before Thanksgiving or after Valentine's Day.

In the north, if you accidentally bump into someone in the mall or on the sidewalk, you may get snapped at. In the South, you'll most likely get an apology, a smile and maybe even a conversation in which you find that you have mutual friends or that you are distantly related.

No reception, tea or social is complete without cucumber sandwiches (with the bread cut into rounds, the same size as the paper-thin slice of cucumber).

Good Southern folk know when and where the Confederate States Cavalry defeated the U.S. Navy.

"Fine sewing" (fancy needlework) is still so very fine.

Keep ingredients on hand for a quick casserole, a pot of soup, or a congealed salad. You never know when someone might be in need of comfort food.

Be patient when yankees, referring to the Southern staple, Silver Queen, ask the silly question, "So how do you guys bleach your corn?"

Remember that in most places a skunk is a polecat, but in Georgia, a skunk is a Sherman.

One Southerner is a person, two are a pair, and three Southerners are a party!

Develop a sense of humor and use it often. The Bible says, "a merry heart doeth good like a medicine."

Love your hometown . . . know its history, its strengths, its beauty. Be proud of where you are from.

Finger bowls (thank goodness) are making a comeback.

On the matter of agitation . . . a temper tantrum is a temper tantrum, and hoppin' mad is hoppin' mad, but a hissy fit is a sight to behold. When someone pitches a 24 carat hissy fit, it usually means that in addition to being as hot as a firecracker, she also stomped her foot and probably threw something.

Once a belle, always a belle!

Know what a football mum is and why it is worn on only one day of the year.

Those "not from here" are quite surprised to find they can't drive on Southern snow either . . . the ice beneath it takes you wherever it wants you to go.

To keep squirrels and other critters out of flower beds, sprinkle cayenne pepper liberally . . . it really cooks as a 'pest'-icide.

Drive to the beach via Alabama and buy some boiled peanuts by the roadside to eat along the way.

Southerners have a special relationship with their iced tea (or sweet tea). As the year-round beverage of choice, it must be strong, full of sugar, and so cold it hurts your teeth.

Southern masculinity has no counterpart, no equal . . . a very secure feeling for the rest of us!

Learn the difference between a fox hound and a coon hound.

Texans like everything in large size, including their generosity.

Serenity is a part of life below the Mason-Dixon line; while frenzy often reigns above it.

Southern ladies love Southern nights with their Southern knights.

Mediocrity is the enemy. Excellence starts with a fire in the heart. Light from that fire flushes out the shadows of mediocrity.

Many Southerners long for a calmer lifestyle, a slower pace, like the days of the old South, but with indoor plumbing.

Class has nothing to do with money, money has nothing to do with class. If you don't have it, you can't buy it.

A gentleman goes about the business of being a gentleman in a quiet way, never with flamboyance.

We are a people yet! (Thank you, Alfred Lord Tennyson.)

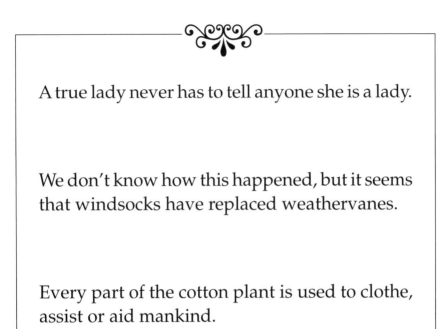

A true lady never has to tell anyone she is a lady.

We don't know how this happened, but it seems that windsocks have replaced weathervanes.

Every part of the cotton plant is used to clothe, assist or aid mankind.

Never, ever put dark meat in your chicken salad.

Southerners may indulge their desires, but never to excess.

Know the meaning of "tacky" and avoid people who are.

Southerners like their rock music with heavy bass, their country music with a twang, and their classical music with a lilt. No wonder we dance our way through life.

Gentlemen, understand that when a lady returns home from a day at the mall with ten full shopping bags, and explains to the gentleman's raised eyebrows, "Dillard's was having a sale," doesn't mean that she bought only sale items or that she shopped only at Dillard's.

Genealogical research is a Southern obsession.

Yankees keep asking why we still fight The War. It's because they came back!

Southern ladies are accused of flirting to get their way . . . we have no further comment about that.

The Southern mystique has led many a scholar to distraction, many a social analyst to tranquilizers, and many an arrow off course.

When a Southerner tells someone to "make yourself at home," he means it.

For a number of reasons we can be thankful we live in the Bible Belt instead of the Beltway.

Whine if you need to, but never through your nose . . . someone might think you're a yankee.

The Southern Table Food Rule: It is better to have *much more* than enough, rather than not enough.

Southerners are naturally polite. It comes from self-contentment and a genuine concern for others.

If Southerners move more slowly, it is to savor the moment.

If your family owns an antique christening gown for its infants, you are very fortunate. If it doesn't, provide one for the future babies to wear and pass down.

Southern mothers teach their daughters to blend gentleness with fine-spun ribbons of steel.

Be a good neighbor. Keep your yard neat, your house in good repair, and your dog out of neighborhood gardens.

If you really need to get after someone, go about it like "a duck on a June bug," or like Forrest after Streight!

Southern snippiness happens occasionally, but is never directed toward your family members . . . it just isn't done.

Remember . . . some things we've taken hold of for the sake of convenience; other things we must hold onto in spite of the inconvenience.

Southerners believe that if "the body is a temple," it should not be allowed to look like a shack.

The oft-used terms, "honey," "darlin," and "sugar," bring a smile to the face and warmth to the heart.

Don't rush and hurry through life . . . like homemade yeast bread, some of the best things take time.

The words "please" and "thank you" are as natural to us as breathing.

Count your Southern blessings every day.

Southern hospitality has been complimented throughout the world, and all the accolades still don't do it justice.

Dancing has always been a vital part of the Southern social scene. In fact, it is almost a faux pas to not know how to move to the music.

Afternoon tea and the wearing of hats bring out the grace that naturally resides within Southerners.

Pick your battles. Attend at least one reenactment of The War each year.

Southerners are hooked on detail – in style of dress, entertaining, home decor, and each other's personal lives.

Don't drink anything called "pop." Always ask for the real thing . . . Coca-Cola.

Southerners agree with Dorothy (of The Wizard of Oz fame) . . . "there's no place like home."

Southerners have a built-in radar (instinct) to find one another when travelling outside the South . . . we're pulled to one another like magnets to steel.

For many generations our ancestors were agrarians.

Learn the difference between "wet ribs" and "dry ribs." (You may have to experiment for a while to make sure.)

Family gatherings in the South can involve meticulous details and planning, but in reality, consist of three basic elements: feasting, storytelling and affection.

The South is its own place and lives in its own time.

Southerners know which personality type you're referring to when you describe someone as "just dripping with snake oil."

The child who prefers to sit with the adults at family gatherings and listen to the stories, rather than go out and play with the other children, will probably become the family historian.

In the South, passion rules . . . whatever lights the inner-fire gets the most attention.

The old custom of thumping a watermelon works. If it doesn't sound hollow, don't buy it . . . its too pulpy.

Farms on Southern hills are plowed in juxtaposition curves to keep our topsoil from taking a ride to the Gulf.

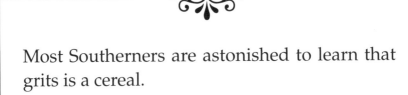

Most Southerners are astonished to learn that grits is a cereal.

Many so-called educational programs on television are bad for Southern children, especially the language portions where they teach the little ones to say "tan" for the number "ten." (Thank you, Michael A. Grissom.)

Many famous Southern singers got their starts in church choirs.

For many good and cherished reasons, Nashville *is* the "Athens of the South."

Gather your friends and sponsor a Confederate unit in your local Veterans Day Parade.

Keep our bardic ways intact. Pass the stories down to each generation, for ours is a unique heritage that deserves to be remembered.

Be confident that no place on earth grows tomatoes and strawberries like Tennessee.

See to it that at sometime in their childhood, all children get to experience the sheer pleasure of holding and petting Beagle puppies.

Make a habit of protesting the fact that in many cases, "multiculturalism" and "diversity" include everyone but native Southerners.

South refers to a state of mind, a place of grace, a way of life, while north, east and west are just directions.

Know that "old times there are not forgotten" . . . we revere the past.

Often the softest voice is the most commanding.

The UDC was organized in Nashville in 1894, and its headquarters are now in Richmond, Virginia. The SCV was organized in Richmond, in 1896, and its headquarters are now in Columbia, Tennessee, near Nashville.

Front porch sitters probably originated in the South.

We can't decide which plague is the worst . . . kudzu, mosquitoes or scalawags.

Don't send invitations or thank-you notes by e-mail. Not only is it impolite, but it gives the recipient about the same feeling as being handed a melted popsicle.

Any Southerner knows the difference between a rascal, a punk and a scoundrel.

Become a tax protester. If you have to ask why, you need to study the reasons for the conflicts of 1776 and 1861.

Louisiana is the place to go for "hot." Where else can you get food, music, and atmosphere so full of fire?

Southern pride – have it, keep it, showcase it!

Sisters, brothers and cousins make excellent best friends. Besides sharing many of the same experiences and adventures, they know you through and through and like you anyway.

Believe it or not, Baptists are allowed to partake of "pot likker."

Know the name, rank, company and regiment of your Confederate ancestors.

Know your Confederate symbols. There is more than one Confederate Flag; the Great Seal of the Confederacy features a hero from another war; and the CSA generals' uniforms incorporated the laurel wreath of ancient Greece.

Most Southerners go to church. Most take it seriously. Most are at peace inside.

Understand that the pea-green color of envy doesn't look good on anyone.

South Carolina may have its walled gardens in Charleston, but its hearts are open to all.

Forget baseball. In the South *football* is the national sport.

Try some Tennessee wines . . . yes, Tennessee. The hills produce rivals to anything from Europe.

Pretty eyes and dimples exist in abundance in the South.

Southerners understand exactly who you mean when you refer to "Mama and Daddy and them."

Know why the Great Smoky Mountains are smoky.

A Southern male knows where and what Camp Forrest was. In fact, many folks do . . . it was the last "touch of home" many men experienced before being shipped overseas to fight in WWII.

Only a Southerner can understand directions from a Southerner. Yankees and others will drive around and around the same route or end up three towns from where they meant to be. You know, if we plan ahead and work it just right . . . maybe. . .

There is a reason why all spacecraft is launched from the South. It is the same reason why everyone wants to come here.

Dare to defend your Southern heritage.

We don't have to wish we were in the "land of cotton" . . . gratefully, it belongs to us.

Southern charm is an inherited trait, as much so as the color of eyes or hair.

The chivalric code may have gone out of style elsewhere, but it is still alive and well and practiced daily in the South.

Southern fathers teach their sons to protect and care for what belongs to them.

A mint julep is to the South what sherry is to England. Riding to the hounds is the same for both.

Offer to give a program or two for your favorite school on the *true* history of the South, because it cannot be found in the textbooks.

One of a belle's most important duties in life is choosing a silver pattern.

When you see a grown man parading the city streets of the South, wearing Bermuda shorts, and black knee socks with sandals, be certain you have come across one of "those people" from "up there."

If you don't know who "The Wizard of the Saddle" was then you probably need to head back over that famous line.

A Southerner always stands his ground; at the same time he always maintains his grace. (Thank you, Charles Lunsford.)

Be above pettiness and don't condescend to contradict gossip. Trying to correct either just adds fuel to the fire.

Anyone who thinks Las Vegas is a busy place probably has never been in the South during the week before a Tennessee-Alabama football game.

Southerners don't normally go in for the new age diets of seeds and twigs, but we sure know about alfalfa sprouts . . . don't we have the healthiest cows in the country?

There are debutante balls all over the South, but one of the most exclusive is the SCV's. Money (old or new) or politics might buy your way into some deb circles, but the only way into the SCV's Debutante Ball is through the proven bloodlines of members.

Own some wicker or rattan furniture for your veranda, patio, portico, porch or sun room.

Obey leash laws for your cat. Your neighbors will love you for it.

Little Southern children are always pretty, whether they are girls or boys.

Hugging is a national pasttime in the South.

The old saying is true . . . "If you've made it (been accepted) in Columbus, Mississippi, you've made it in the whole South."

Nothing can startle one out of complacency or a deep sleep like a booming, crackling Southern thunderstorm.

Nowhere do copy machines get a workout (and overload) like the ones in the Libraries and Archives of Southern states.

If you visit California, don't order barbecue for dinner, even if the sign says, "Old Time Southern Barbeque," . . . even if the waitress says the owner is from Georgia.

Southern cuisine reflects not only the wide variety of fare available, but also the abundance of it.

Deviled eggs must be served on a deviled-egg plate; anything else will turn them into "scrambled eggs."

Invest in the best and most luxurious table linens and bedroom linens you can afford. After all, many of life's most tender and important moments take place among those linens.

Southerners are survivors.

If you are an Episcopalian, attend Midnight Mass on Christmas Eve (the most beautiful service of the year). If you're not, ask an Episcopalian to take you along.

Don't believe the northern myth that the South is better off to have lost The War.

It drives Southern men crazy that their ladies don't look under the hood before they buy a car. Why should we. . . . we know they'll check it out five times for us!

Call foundation blocks by their best-known name . . . Breeko Blocks, not concrete blocks.

The appliance that keeps your food cold should be called an icebox.

Always offer both kinds of slaw (vinegar and mayonnaise) when serving barbecue or catfish.

Attend the Fiddlers' Convention in Mt. Airy, North Carolina. It will entertain you, fill your ears with mountain music, and cause your feet to do things you didn't know they could do.

Know which Southern animal wears a mask and which one carries a flag.

Southern gentlemen are confident enough in their masculinity that they can attend Opening Night at the Ballet on Friday, then be wrapped in camouflage and in the deer stand before daylight on Saturday.

If you don't know who the Daughters and the Sons are, then you are probably "not from here."

Southerners are richly blessed to have been born of this land and tenderly reared on the traditions that make us a unique people in a special place.

Southern writers take paragraph breaks (but usually just for iced tea).

While belles often don't like to clean (there may be a little dust on the dining room table) you can be sure that the silver in the sideboard is polished to a high sheen.

The St. Andrews Cross, named for the patron saint of Scotland, has appeared on numerous flags between the Battle of Bannockburn in 1314, and The War Between the States in the 1860s. It has hovered over the Celtic people as a badge of honor for many generations.

Southerners like to feed people. Doing so nourishes the soul of the giver.

Southerners "still smell the powder burning." (Thank you, Shenandoah.)

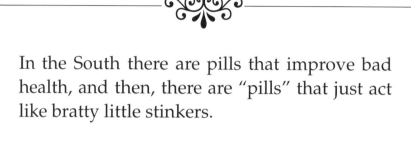

In the South there are pills that improve bad health, and then, there are "pills" that just act like bratty little stinkers.

Know how a mule gets to be a mule.

The secret Southern ladies know is that if the men are happy, everyone is happy . . . they return the favors.

Southerners don't mind laughing at themselves . . . they're not so "touchy" as some groups.

Southern ladies own at least one bed jacket.

Southern men usually suffer from one or both afflictions: mall dread and remote-controlitis.

Homemade ice cream just tastes better.

The oldest sorority in the nation is Alpha Delta Pi, founded in 1851, at Wesleyan Female College in Macon, Georgia. First called the Adelphean Society, it was nationally recognized in 1904 and changed the name to Alpha Delta Phi, then the Phi to Pi, to avoid confusion with a men's organization. It is one of the largest and most active sororities in the world.

Southern ladies, without uttering a cross word, can "freeze" to the core someone who has breached the codes of conduct of polite society.

The first known Christmas tree on this continent was erected and decorated in the South, of course. In 1842, a German-born teacher at William and Mary College, in Williamsburg, asked permission of a friend to prepare a Christmas tree for his children. A party was planned around the decorating of the tree. A tradition was born, and with it inventive decorations, as Southerners made tree trimmings for many years from materials on hand.

Southerners are loving and giving.

Many Southerners believe that Santa Claus is a Confederate. (Thank you, Charlie Andrews.)

Arkansas folks know why Helena is such an important town.

If you are "not from here" one of the best ways to fit in is to forget that you just moved here from wherever, and most of all to forget "how you did things up there."

At fast food restaurants keep asking for French fries . . . fries can be many things . . . with French fries you know you're getting potatoes.

Southerners are nourished by their land . . . physically and mentally.

Remember that the first "thanksgiving" was held in Jamestown, Virginia, not in Plymouth, Mass., as we were taught in school.

Southerners always greet one another with effervescence.

We love to celebrate, and any occasion will do . . . after all, we are the descendants of the Cavaliers.

A true Southern lady wears stockings with dresses, even in the summer in the middle of a heat wave.

Don't let the proximity to D.C. fool you . . . Virginia is still Virginia, and proud of it.

Never let anyone make you feel ashamed of being a Southerner.

In the South, history is not some old, worn tale of how things were . . . it is a guide and an inspiration for the future.

Ladies, accept the fact that he will clean all of his guns before a hunting trip, using all manner of cloths, tools, oils and waxes. He will polish them, groom them, lock, stock and barrel, metal and wood. But, in the kitchen, he will never warm to the concept of using steel wool on pots and pans.

When Southerners want a sweet treat they either indulge in baby talk (Goo Goo) or call for the mighty king of the jungle (King Leo Peppermint Sticks).

Southerners believe good government is run by "the consent of the governed."

If your biscuits regularly come from a can, perhaps your life is a little too hectic.

Know the meaning of the term, "kissin' cousin," and whether or not you have one.

The songs of the South are born in the hearts of those who till the land.

A true Southerner knows which of many wars The War is.

No one can flounce out of a room and slam the door like a true Southern belle.

The favorite summer treat is a tomato sandwich. Or two.

Okra can appear on the table boiled, batter-fried, pickled, or dried as a part of the centerpiece.

A good Southerner knows what early rock and roll song and what Memphis cosmetics company share the same name.

Always serve black-eyed peas (cooked with hog jowl) on New Year's Day to have "good luck" throughout the New Year.

In rural areas and small towns everyone nods and waves as you pass by. You should always return the nod and wave.

Some folks think your work, career, job, etc., is just what you do to support your *real life* – being Southern and enjoying it immensely.

Corporations could learn a lot about communication from Southern waitresses . . . a smiling face, a cheerful voice, a helpful attitude, so that even when the restaurant has sold completely out of country ham and grits, the message is delivered, coated in so much honey, the diner believes he really, all the time, wanted fried chicken and green beans, anyway.

Never question a Southerner when you're told, "We're doing it that way because that's the way it has always been done."

Being Southern means belonging; it means always having backup support; it means your place within the group is always *yours*.

Flower gardens are profuse in the South, with many gardeners exchanging seeds, cuttings and bulbs. In fact, Mrs. R. E. Lee made a habit of taking specially-loved specimens from her garden at Arlington and planting them wherever her husband's military career took them . . . a touch of home in new surroundings.

Many folks think the daytime sky is bluer in the South, and the nighttime sky is brighter.

What a surprise! Now experiencing a "revival" in the home furnishings industry is the dressing table . . . that essential piece of furniture that holds the elements of appearance and pampering so dear to the hearts of Southern ladies. One more reason the South was right!

The Tennessee Walking Horse has fine, strong bones, the result of a diet rich in the limestone-fed bluegrass of Tennessee and Kentucky.

There's rock and roll, rock-a-bye-baby, and rock and blues . . . and then there is Southern Rock . . . a music form which has defied description, caused dancers to defy gravity, and caused Baby Boomers to defy their parents' orders to "turn that racket down!" And Southern Boomers are still known to crank it up to top volume when they hear the beat kick in, and the Allman Brothers start to growl out, "I got one more silver dollar, and I'm not gonna let 'em catch me, no, not gonna let 'em catch the Midnight Rider."

Laughter (and lots of it) is the oil on which the South runs so smoothly.

When the dust finally settles from our techno-driven entry into this new millennium (probably about 2050) The South will still be here, gracious, accommodating, noble, and still serving sweet tea.

If Southerners are still "fighting the war," our best weapons are pen and paper, a voice reinforced by a mind filled with truth, and the determination to never back up.

Southerners have a flair for the dramatic . . . it puts the "icing on the cake."

A prominent fraternity, Kappa Alpha, went through several name changes, first Phi Kappa Psi, then to avoid confusion with another fraternity, to the letters K. A., then to the Kappa Alpha Order. Greatly influenced by the life and character of Robert E. Lee, who was, after The War, President of Washington University, home of Kappa Alpha, the fraternity has served the nation in many charitable ways.

Nothing warms away winter's chill like a handmade quilt.

Southerners, returning home after having lived away from here, have been known to stop the car just over the state line, get out, kneel, and kiss the ground of the first Southern state they drive into.

When "the girls" get together, they talk and discuss and elaborate and talk some more – about fashion, entertainment, family, and most of all, the men. When "the men" get together, they discuss a little business, a little sports, maybe some current events, then spend the rest of the time wondering what on earth "the girls" have to talk about all that time!

On a soft summer night turn off the television, go outside with the children, and watch them catch lightening bugs, while you listen to their laughter above the pleasant sounds of nature.

One of nature's most calming sounds is the rhythm of the ocean lapping Florida's sandy shores.

Never wear white to a wedding unless you are the bride.

Some of the elderly Southern ladies are alarmed by today's casual style of living and dress. Certain the country is going downhill, they note that: three of the communicants that sit on the pew in front of them regularly wear sweats to church; the new clerk at the bakery never says, "here you are, Miss Catherine, or Miss Eugenia" but instead yells out, "here's yah order;" and the beauty shop where they have gone for forty-five years has stopped using rollers and gone to gel.

Understand that only a Southern-born mouth can speak with a true Southern drawl.

If the South could be described in one word, that word would be *"integrity."*

The South, the South . . . we are smitten with this place.

Believe us when we say that we will never give up our way of life, and we will always sing *Dixie*.